Test Your Vocabulary – Book 4

Peter Watcyn-Jones

Illustrated by Sven Nordqvist

PENGUIN BOOKS

PENGUIN BOOKS

Published by the Penguin Group
27 Wrights Lane, London W8 5TZ, England
Viking Penguin Inc., 40 West 23rd Street, New York, New York 10010, USA
Penguin Books Australia Ltd, Ringwood, Victoria, Australia
Penguin Books Canada Ltd, 2801 John Street, Markham, Ontario, Canada L3R 1B4
Penguin Books (NZ) Ltd, 182–190 Wairau Road, Auckland 10, New Zealand

Penguin Books Ltd, Registered Offices: Harmondsworth, Middlesex, England

First published in Sweden by Kursverksamhetens förlag 1983
Published in Penguin Books 1985
10 9 8 7 6

Text copyright © Peter Watcyn-Jones, 1983
Illustrations copyright © Sven Nordqvist, 1983
All rights reserved

Made and printed in Great Britain by
Hazell Watson & Viney Limited
Member of BPCC Limited
Aylesbury, Bucks, England
Set in Times

INTRODUCTION

Owing to the emphasis in recent years on functional and communicative approaches to language learning, many other important areas of the language have been neglected. One such area is vocabulary. This series is an attempt to remedy this situation not only by filling a real gap in the materials available but also by attempting to show that vocabulary learning can be just as much fun and just as stimulating as other activities. There are five books altogether in the series, ranging from Elementary level to Advanced. Each book contains fifty tests or exercises and, to facilitate self-study, a key is also included. Students using these books should find vocabulary learning both stimulating and enjoyable and, hopefully, start to develop a real sensitivity to the language.

Test Your Vocabulary – Book 4 is the final book in the series and is intended for advanced students – in particular students studying for the Cambridge Proficiency or similar examinations or University students. It is similar to *Test Your Vocabulary – Book 3* and contains, among other things, further tests on word-building and phrasal verbs. In addition, there are tests based on different ways of saying the same thing, slang and colloquial expressions. There are approximatley 800 words in the book.

TO THE STUDENT

This book will help you to learn a lot of new English words. But in order for the new words to become "fixed" in your mind, you need to test yourself again and again. Here is one method you can use to help you learn the words:

1. Read through the instructions carefully for the test you are going to try. Then try the test, writing your answers **in pencil**.
2. When you have finished, check your answers and correct any mistakes you have made. Read through the test again, paying special attention to the words you didn't know or got wrong.
3. Try the test again five minutes later. You can do this either by covering up the words (for example, in the picture tests) or by asking a friend to test you. Repeat this until you can remember all the words.
4. **Rub out your answers.**
5. Try the test again the following day. (You should remember most of the words.)
6. Finally, plan to try the test at least twice again within the following month. After this most of the words will be "fixed" in your mind.

CONTENTS

1 The animal kingdom

Write the number of each drawing next to the correct word.

bat	5
donkey	8
octopus	11
wolf	6
elk	3
fox	9
rhinoceros	12
hedgehog	1
reindeer	7
hippopotamus	1
squirrel	10
tortoise	4

2 Missing words – Travel, etc.

Put the following words into the correct sentences. Use each word once only.

flight	travel	run
journey	voyage	cruise
trip	outing	package tour
excursion	tour	expedition

1 We visited lots of famous towns on our American .... last year.

2 Before the invention of the aeroplane, the .... from Britain to America could take weeks, even months sometimes.

3 Do you want to come for a .... in my new car on Sunday?

4 The plane now arriving is .... SAS 343 from Copenhagen.

5 The first thing I did when I got to London was to go on a sightseeing ....

6 In my opinion, the best way to .... is by air.

7 Last summer I stayed in Brighton and one day our group went on a very interesting .... to Blenheim Palace, the home of the late Winston Churchill.

8 My uncle is going on an .... next year to try to discover the lost city of Atlantis.

9 How long does the train .... from London to Edinburgh take?

10 Last year my mother went on a Mediterranean .... and was seasick practically the whole time.

11 One of the main advantages of going on a ...., apart from the price, is the fact that you don't have to spend weeks beforehand planning routes, finding hotels, buying air tickets, etc. It's all done for you.

12 We went on a day's .... to the zoo in Copenhagen and the whole family loved it.

3 Choose the word 1

Choose the word which best completes each sentence.

1 He used to observe the stars from his attic through the ....
    a roof window   b cupola   c skylight   d French windows
    e attic window

2 Excuse me, John, do you think I could .... your phone?
    a use   b lend   c borrow   d take
    e loan

3 I'm sorry, David. It wasn't my .... to cause a quarrel between you and Joanna.
    a meaning   b point   c intention   d view
    e reason

4 Although someone had seen him take the watch, he still .... it.
    a refused   b rejected   c disowned   d denied
    e hid

5 The inside of an apple is called the ....
    a pip   b core   c stone   d peel
    e kernel

6 A woman who has never married is called a ....
    a virgin   b widower   c bachelor   d spinster
    e widow

7 In England, it is easy to drive at night because of the .... along the middle of the road.
    a cat's eyes   b lines   c signposts   d indicators
    e warning lights

8 The .... between the rich and poor countries of the world is increasing daily.
    a space   b gap   c distance   d interval
    e opening

9 Before every Board Meeting, it is customary for the .... of the previous meeting to be read out.
    a   protocol   b   notes   c   précis   d   minutes
    e   points

10 On first coming to England, I fell .... in love with a girl who lived in the flat below mine.
    a   feet over hands   b   hole over hole   c   foot in mouth   d   elbow to toe
    e   head over heels

11 A cat licks its .... before it washes its face.
    a   paw   b   hoof   c   tail   d   claws
    e   fur

12 I'm afraid I haven't the .... idea why he never turned up.
    a   least   b   faintest   c   weakest   d   fainted
    e   simplest

13 I badly .... my ankle when I fell on my way home last night.
    a   stretched   b   sprained   c   strained   d   pulled
    e   caught

14 People are .... to wear reflectors on their clothing when walking along a road in the dark.
    a   told   b   warned   c   advised   d   suggested
    e   informed

15 I'm not surprised he became an author. Even as a child he had a .... imagination.
    a   large   b   great   c   vivid   d   bright
    e   clean

16 The TV announcer apologized for the breakdown and said that normal service would be .... as soon as possible.
    a   resumed   b   returned   c   continuous   d   repeated
    e   recovered

17 I hate .... oranges. I usually get my wife to do it for me since she has long nails.
    a   skinning   b   slicing   c   peeling   d   shaving
    e   cutting

18 My mother was .... ill last summer but, fortunately, is now
making a slow but steady recovery.
  a critically   b deeply   c fatally   d definitely
  e serious

19 You haven't seen my knitting .... anywhere, have you? I
can't seem to find them.
  a pins   b nails   c rods   d sticks
  e needles

20 Mr and Mrs Grove were very .... when their dog died.
  a anxious   b upset   c confused   d disappointed
  e discouraged

4 Phrasal verbs 1

Replace the words in brackets in the following sentences with a suitable phrasal verb. (Make any other necessary changes).

call on	get down	cut up
get on for	go off	take off
do in	look in	go down with
turn down	take to	go out
go down	get at	give away
look up	go back to	take away

1 If he says that again I'll .... him .... — I swear it!
　　　　　　　　　　　　　(kill him)

2 You'd better not drink that milk, Joe. It's ....
　　　　　　　　　　　　　　　　(turned sour)

3 We knew he wasn't English as his accent .... him
　　　　　　　　　　　　　　　　　　(betrayed him)

....

4 The house I live in .... the 15th century.
　　　　　　(dates from)

5 Let's .... Paul and Jan tonight. It's been ages since
　　(go and visit)

we last saw them.

6 Clive was really .... when he failed his proficiency
　　　　　　　　(upset)

exam.

7 I think I'll go somewhere for the weekend. Things have been ....

me .... lately, so a change of air will do me good.
(making me depressed)

8 John can't come with us tonight after all. It seems he's ....
　　　　　　　　　　　　　　　　　　　(caught)

a cold.

9 "What does 'misogynist' mean, Allan?"

"I've no idea, Jill. You'd better .... it .... in the diction-
　　　　　　　　　　(find out its meaning)

ary.

10 The power point was behind the piano, which made it very difficult to

.... (reach)

11 You're not going to wear a mini-skirt are you, Jane? They

.... years ago.
   (stopped being fashionable)

12 "How old is Eva?"

"I'm not sure, but she must be .... forty."
                              (nearly)

13 If you .... 25 from 100, you're left with 75.
         (subtract)

14 No one really believed it when the news came through that the "Titanic" had

.... on her maiden voyage.
(sunk)

15 I tried smoking a pipe once, but I never really .... it.
                                              (liked)

16 I was offered a job in Leeds but I .... it .... because I
                                    (refused it)

didn't want to move away from Hastings.

17 I can't stop now but I'll .... later on my way home
                          (pay a short visit)

from work.

18 You should see Brian .... the new boss. The way he
                       (imitate)

does it is really fantastic. He's just like him!

7

5 Definitions – Types of people

Fill in the missing words in the definitions below. Choose from the following:

chauvinistic	versatile	gullible
illiterate	magnanimous	vivacious
bilingual	indefatigable	convivial
erudite	scintillating	greedy

1 A/an .... person is someone who has a variety of skills and abilities and who is able to change easily from one sort of activity to another.

2 A/an .... person is someone who is very friendly and fond of eating, drinking and good company.

3 A/an .... person is someone who is very generous towards other people.

4 A/an .... person is someone who always wants more than his or her fair share of something—especially food, money or power.

5 A/an .... person is someone who is easily taken in or tricked by others.

6 A/an .... person is someone who believes that the sex he or she belongs to (male or female) is better than the opposite sex in all ways.

7 A/an .... person is someone who is unable to read or write.

8 A/an .... person is someone who is fluent in two languages.

9 A/an .... person is someone who seems to have so much energy that he or she never tires.

10 A/an .... person is someone who has studied a lot and is very knowledgeable.

11 A/an .... person is someone who is able to make clever, witty and entertaining remarks or conversation.

12 A/an .... person is someone (usually a woman) who is full of life.

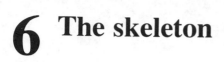

6 The skeleton

Write the numbers 1–12 next to the correct word or words.

thigh bone	. . . . .
collarbone	. . . . .
kneecap	. . . . .
skull	. . . . .
shin bone (tibia)	. . . . .
wrist bones	. . . . .
breastbone	. . . . .
spine/backbone	. . . . .
shoulder blade	. . . . .
hipbone	. . . . .
fibula	. . . . .
rib	. . . . .

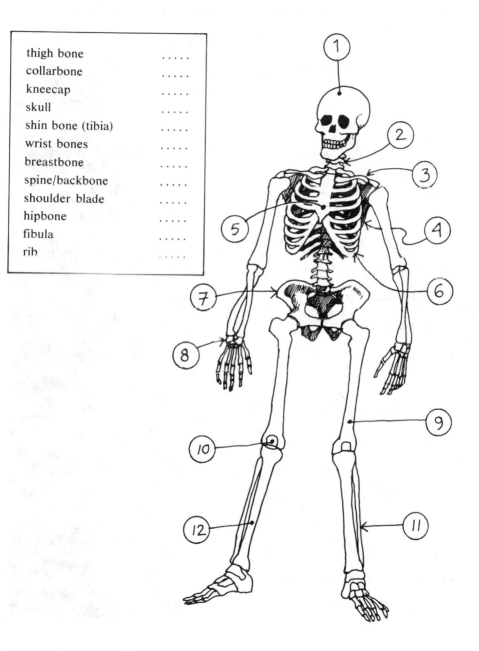

7 Word association

The following groups of four words are all connected with the same thing. Write down the missing word in each group. Before starting, look at the example.

Example: bark, trunk, leaf, branch TREE

1 cell, warder, sentence, bars

2 key, hammer, grand, pedal

3 column, circulation, tabloid, article

4 springs, head, foot, sheet

5 green, hole, swing, club

6 hood, hub cap, bonnet, wing

7 zodiac, moon, Mars, Sagittarius

8 corner, ring, second, bout

9 hand, strap, wind, time

10 tile, gutter, chimney, skylight

11 paw, fur, whiskers, claws

12 lens, shutter, speed, flash

13 circle, stalls, auditorium, box office

14 wing, tail, undercarriage, fly

15 frame, pane, catch, glass

16 coffin, wreath, cemetery, corpse

17 pawn, castle, bishop, queen

18 moat, battlements, keep, dungeon

19 scrum, try, All Blacks, line-out

20 cowshed, pen, barn, harvest

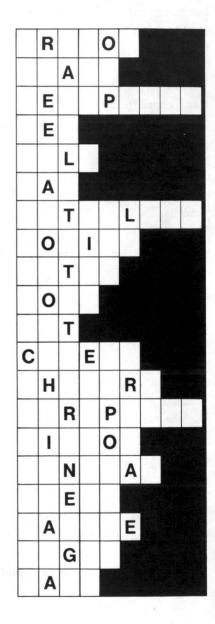

8 Missing words – Nature, etc.

Put the following words into the correct sentences. Use each word once only.

countryside	country	setting
nature	bush	scene
landscape	scenery	rural
view	highlands	environment

1 Many people choose Switzerland for their holidays because of its beautiful

....

2 Turner was one of England's most famous .... painters.

3 They stood gazing at the happy .... of children playing in the park.

4 If I had to choose, I would much prefer to live in the .... than in a town.

5 One of the most beautiful and unspoilt areas of Britain are the .... of Scotland.

6 The main difference between the English and French .... is that in England most fields and meadows are bordered by hedges, giving the impression from a distance of a large patchwork quilt.

7 Children living in .... areas often have to travel miles to school every day.

8 One of the most frightening examples of the force of .... is seen during a tornado.

9 In Australia, the name given to the wild, uncleared area of the country is the

....

10 The house, standing alone in the middle of the marsh, was the perfect .... for a horror film.

11 Many people are very concerned with the way Man has destroyed and continues to destroy the ....

12 Although I liked the appearance of the house, what really made me decide to buy it was the fantastic .... through the window.

9 Word building 1

The word in capitals at the end of each of the following sentences can be used to form a word that fits suitably in the blank space. Fill each blank in this way.

Example: You can always rely on Barbara. She is very
      DEPENDABLE   DEPEND

1 He was born blind; but despite this .... ABLE
   he still managed to become one of the top Pop singers of
   his generation.

2 .... I'm in favour of the plan, but BASE
   there are still one or two points that I'm not entirely happy
   with.

3 What a lovely painting! Your daughter must be very ART
   ...., Mrs Green.

4 I think it's very .... of him to REASON
   expect us to work overtime every night this week.

5 There is a saying in English: "................................. ACT
   speak louder than words."

6 That rule is not .... in this case. APPLY

7 I don't think Tom's been getting too much sleep lately. His BLOOD
   eyes are terribly ....

8 English is a .... easy language for COMPARE
   Swedes to learn.

9 Now, don't tell anyone else what I've just told you. Re- CONFIDE
   member, it's ....

10 I don't think their marriage will last long. They're CONTINUE
   .... quarrelling.

11 The teacher punished the child for .... OBEY

12 Librarians spend a lot of their time .... CLASS
   books.

13 I don't care if you'd had too much to drink. Your be- DEFEND
   haviour last night was quite ....

14 If you think I'm going to marry you, then I'm afraid you're   TAKE
   very much ....

15 The man was found guilty of fraud and sentenced to three   PRISON
   years ....

16 Despite the star-studded cast, the film was only ....   PART
   .... successful.

17 He won the discus event at the Olympic Games but was   QUALIFY
   later .... when a medical check
   proved that he had been taking drugs.

18 The recent hurricane caused ....   WIDE
   damage.

19 Industrial robots work with far greater ....   PRECISE
   than most men.

20 I've tried to advise my daughter against hitch-hiking   HEAD
   around Europe alone, but she won't listen to me. She's so

   ....

10 Synonyms and opposites crossword: adjectives

Read through the sentences below and fill in the crossword.

ACROSS

1 Synonym for unbelievable
2 Synonym for hard-working
3 Opposite of generous
4 Synonym for thoughtful
5 Synonym for impolite
6 Opposite of permanent
7 Opposite of sharp
8 Opposite of modest
9 Opposite of deliberate
10 Synonym for enormous

DOWN

1 Synonym for annoyed
2 Opposite of opaque
3 Synonym for stubborn
4 Synonym for peculiar
5 Opposite of plentiful
6 Opposite of voluntary
7 Opposite of gigantic
8 Synonym for wealthy
9 Synonym for reliable
10 Synonym for thrilling

11 Missing words – Ways of looking

Put the following words into the correct sentences. Use each word once only and make any necessary changes.

distinguish	recognise	gaze	eye
scrutinise	watch	notice	catch a glimpse of
glance	stare	catch someone's eye	glare
peer	peep	observe	look at

1 He had changed so much since I last saw him that I hardly .... him.

2 The young girl .... lovingly at the photograph of her boyfriend.

3 I only .... him, so I can't really remember whether he was wearing a hat or not.

4 As my brother is colour-blind, he finds it difficult to .... between green and blue.

5 "................................... the board, please!" said the teacher.

6 She .... out of the window for a moment, then carried on working.

7 The old man .... through the closed curtains at his new neighbours.

8 The teacher .... angrily at the class. "For the last time, who broke the window?" she roared.

9 He .... the figures very carefully before making any comment.

10 In Britain it is considered rude to .... at people.

11 The policeman .... the young man suspiciously.

12 He .... through the thick fog, trying to make out the number of the approaching bus.

13 I waved to attract her attention, but she walked away without .... me.

14 Are you going to .... the film on TV tonight?

15 I wanted to order coffee, but the waiter was so busy that it was very difficult to ....

16 When I was a student, I used to spend a lot of time sitting in cafés, ... the way people used their hands when they spoke to one another.

12 Collective nouns

Fill in the missing words.

| | 1 A ..... of actors | 2 A ..... of Indians | 3 A ..... of directors | 4 A ..... of furniture | 5 A ..... of birds | 6 A ..... of grapes | 7 A ..... of puppies | 8 A ..... of football players | 9 A ..... of teachers | 10 A ..... of people | 11 A ..... of cattle | 12 A ..... of bees | 13 A ..... of golf clubs | 14 A ..... of sailors | 15 A ..... of wolves | 16 A ..... of fish | 17 A ..... of ships | 18 A ..... of armour | 19 A ..... of rags | 20 A ..... of steps |

1 A ..... of actors

2 A ..... of Indians

3 A ..... of directors

4 A ..... of furniture

5 A ..... of birds

6 A ..... of grapes

7 A ..... of puppies

8 A ..... of football players

9 A ..... of teachers

10 A ..... of people

11 A ..... of cattle

12 A ..... of bees

13 A ..... of golf clubs

14 A ..... of sailors

15 A ..... of wolves

16 A ..... of fish

17 A ..... of ships

18 A ..... of armour

19 A ..... of rags

20 A ..... of steps

C	O	m	P	a	n	y
		I				
	O					
			T			
	L					
			C			
		T		E		
	E					
		A				
	R					
	E					
S						
	E					
		E				
	A					
S			A			
	L					
S						
		N				
	L					

13 Objects and things in the home

Write the number of each of the following drawings next to the correct word.

nut 2
butter-dish 3
coal scuttle 12
sieve ....
box of tissues ... 10
bolt ....
rubbish-bin ....
washer ....
table-mat ....
chopper ....
draining-board ... .
mantlepiece ....

14 Colloquial expressions 1

Replace the words in brackets in the following sentences with a suitable colloquial expression from the list below.

dead beat	flogging a dead horse	make ends meet
was a bit out of sorts	at loggerheads	got into hot water
gave me the cold shoulder	get a move on	it sticks out a mile
cats and dogs	black and blue all over	hit the roof
hard up	few and far between	stuck up

1 I'm not going to play football again. I was ....
(covered with bruises)

.... after the match last Saturday.

2 I wish I hadn't taken that day off without asking for permission. I really ....
.... when Mr Bradshaw found out.
(got into trouble)

3 I always seem to be .... these days. I can't
(short of money)

even afford to go to the pub at weekends.

4 Charles and his wife are always .... I really
(quarrelling)

don't know why they got married in the first place.

5 I do wish our teacher wouldn't keep telling Jane how good she is. She's getting far
too .... for words!
(conceited)

6 After running 20 kilometres yesterday afternoon I was absolutely ....
(exhausted)

....

7 What's wrong with Sue? I said hello to her but she ....
(completely ignored me)

....

8 What with rising prices and everything, I'm surprised that anyone can ....
.... nowadays.
       (manage financially)

9 My son .... today,
                (wasn't feeling very well)
   so I decided to keep him home from school.

10 You're .... trying to
                (wasting your time)
   persuade Charles to come with us. You know he won't go anywhere without his
   wife.

11 Jill's father .... when she told him that she
                (became very angry)
   had lost his car keys.

12 My visits to my parents nowadays are, unfortunately, very ....
                                                    (infrequent)
   ....

13 Look, if we don't ...., we're going to miss the
                (hurry)
   last bus!

14 Could you lend me an umbrella, Sally? It's raining..
                                                    (heavily)
   at the moment.

15 Of course Peter's in love with Joanna. ....!
                                (It's so obvious)

15 Prepositional phrases 1

Fill in the missing prepositions in the following sentences.

1 Giant pandas rarely breed .... *captivity.*

2 My car's not worth much— .... *most* £50.

3 English people .... *general* are very friendly. .... *least* that's what I've heard.

4 Don't ask Rose to join the choir. She sings .... *tune* all the time.

5 I don't know why they got married. They have absolutely nothing .... *common.*

6 Most Englishmen earn .... *average* about £110 a week.

7 Oh, what's the word? I know it! *It's* .... *the tip* .... *my tongue!*

8 Don't forget that you can always come to me if you're ever .... *trouble.*

9 He died .... *the age* .... eighty-five.

10 Thank you for coming, Mr Baker. We'll be contacting you .... *due course* about our decision.

11 It's my own fault, I suppose. I took him .... *his word* when he said he wouldn't try to run away.

12 The young, inexperienced teacher tried .... *vain* to control her noisy class.

13 I'll overlook it this time, but please try to be more polite .... *future.*

14 To pay 60 % income-tax is .... *no means* unusual in Sweden.

15 My sister plays the piano .... *ear.*

16 The rent is to be paid .... *advance.*

17 He sent the documents to the bank .... *safe keeping.*

18 His name is Nicholas—Nick .... *short.*

19 This book is .... *far* the best one he's ever written.

20 Work on the new motorway is already .... *progress.*

16 Who's the boss?

Choose from the words on the right the name of the person who is in charge of or the leading person in the group, place, etc. on the left. Look at the example first.

1 The British Army	*FIELD MARSHAL*	captain
2 The United Nations		chairman
3 A TV programme		leader
4 A group of workers		matron
5 A shop		chief/chieftain
6 A primary school		governor
7 A monastery		Managing Director
8 A football team		choirmaster
9 A museum		Principal
10 A prison		foreman
11 Servants (in a household)		umpire
12 A college		President
13 A committee		headmaster/
14 A university		headmistress
15 A tennis match		manager
16 The governing party (in Britain)		butler
17 A tribe		Mother Superior
18 A company		Field Marshal
19 A convent		curator
20 An orchestra		warden
21 An Old People's Home		editor
22 A choir		producer
23 A Republic		Vice-Chancellor
24 A newspaper or magazine		abbot
25 A hospital		Secretary-General
		Prime Minister

17 Words associated with numbers

Read through the following sentences and fill in the missing words.

1 In this mathematical system, 101 = 5.

2 A 3-wheeled cycle.

3 A period of a hundred years.

4 One person who sings.

5 A person who has two wives.

6 Two people singing together.

7 A five-sided figure.

8 A period of ten years.

9 An aeroplane with two sets of wings.

10 A period of two weeks.

11 A combat between two people.

12 A dramatic performance or speech for a single actor.

13 A person who can use both hands equally well.

14 Two babies born at the same time.

15 An insect which is said to have a hundred feet.

16 An instrument with two lenses which helps bring distant objects closer.

17 A mythological animal with a horn in the middle of its head.

18 Four musicians playing together.

19 Government by two or more parties.

20 Three babies born at the same time.

18 Confusing words

Choose the correct word in each of the following sentences.

1 Although she was (crippled/lame) and thus confined to a wheelchair, she still managed to cope with a family and most of the housework.

2 The dress doesn't fit. I'll have to have it (changed/altered).

3 If people must smoke in bed, then they should at least take the precaution of buying (non-flammable/inflammable) sheets and blankets.

4 Although my father has (deficient/defective) hearing, he still refuses to wear a hearing-aid.

5 The baby (blinked/winked) when its mother clapped her hands in front of its face.

6 Of all the writers of (comic/comical) opera, Gilbert and Sullivan are my favourites.

7 Where were you (educated/trained) to be a teacher?

8 My brother is studying to be an (electrical/electric) engineer.

9 I do wish you'd grow up, John! You're so (childish/childlike) at times.

10 There's a (rumour/reputation) going round the office that Mr Burgess and Miss Gibson are getting engaged.

11 I wonder if you would like to (co-operate/collaborate) with me on a book I'm thinking of writing about famous women in politics?

12 There is a very good (Technological/Technical) College not far from where I live.

13 Did you know that Peter had arranged the party (specially/especially) for you?

14 I couldn't care less one way or the other. I'm completely (uninterested/disinterested).

15 I hear that Manchester United beat Liverpool two—(nil/nought) in last night's Cup match.

16 There is a very strong (possibility/opportunity) that man will land on the planet Mars before the year 2000.

17 South Wales was once a flourishing coal-mining area, but today there are hundreds of (misused/disused) coalmines scattered throughout the valleys.

18 My uncle has just got a divorce, which is very strange since he is a marriage guidance (councillor/counsellor).

19 I'm afraid the boot is full. There is no (room/space) for any more suitcases.

20 It's much too hot. Let's go and sit in the (shadow/shade) for a while.

21 I'll see you next week—(eventually/possibly) on Friday.

22 The tennis match was held up for ten minutes when the (umpire/referee) fainted.
23 Any idea what the present Government's (politics/policy) is on defence?
24 They climbed up the steep stone (stairs/steps) leading to the old church.
25 I hope he has got a good (solicitor/barrister) to represent him in court. Robbing a bank is a pretty serious offence.
26 What did you think of the (critic/write-up) we got in the paper this morning?
27 His (financial/economic) worries were solved when he suddenly won £250,000 on the Football Pools.
28 During the last war, Vera Lynn's songs contributed greatly to the (morals/morale) of the troops.
29 My new flat is just around the corner from my office, which is very (convenient/comfortable) for me.
30 The house I have just bought is in a very good residential area, close to shops, schools and other local (amenities/facilities).

19 Choose the word 2

Choose the word which best completes each sentence.

1 I'm afraid I really couldn't eat any more. I'm ....
   a full up   b fed up   c filled up   d famished   e satisfactory

2 It's a .... of time talking to James. He never listens.
   a lot   b loss   c slash   d waste   e model

3 Which .... of cigarettes do you usually smoke, Ulla?
   a make   b sort   c mark   d brand   e shortage

4 He was found guilty of having lied when giving evidence in court and, as a result, was sentenced to two years imprisonment for ....
   a fraud   b a liar   c perjury   d deception   e lying

5 Don't tell Allan about John and Mary. You know he can't .... a secret.
   a hold   b keep   c save   d stop   e prevent

6 May I borrow your pen, Jane? I seem to have .... mine at home.
   a left   b forgotten   c lost   d kept   e missed

7 Last year ABBA made a .... of several million crowns.
   a win   b gain   c profit   d salary   e rise

8 Even though I didn't want my son to leave home, since he was twenty-one there was nothing I could do to .... it.
   a hinder   b prevent   c resist   d end   e cease

9 A/an .... five thousand people are believed to have died in the recent earthquake in South America.
   a guessed   b average   c supposed to   d estimated   e approximately

10 You'll have to use the stairs, I'm afraid. The lift is out of ....
   a function   b work   c order   d form   e functioning

11 Have you seen a mug anywhere, Roy? We seem to be one ....
   a missed   b less   c under   d deficient   e short

12 We got a very good .... in the newspaper this morning. They must have liked the play.
   a critic   b article   c advertisement   d write-up   e praise

13 There was a flash of lightning quickly followed by a loud .... of thunder.

a bang b clap c smash d noise e stroke

14 I can't eat this meat; it's too ....

a strong b soggy c tough d bad e tender

15 Is there anything .... you'd like me to do?

a else b more c still d yet e again

16 Don't tell Anne about Paul and Jane breaking up—you know what a/an .... she is; it will be all over the town in no time.

a talker b liar c gossip d scavenger e informer

17 One day I'm going to find a/an .... of land somewhere in the country and build a house on it.

a area b plot c ground d patch e tomb

18 I was caught parking on a double yellow line and had to pay a £5 parking ....

a fine b bait c summons d fee e cost

19 David's married Elizabeth Green? No, I don't believe it! You're pulling my ....!

a toe b leg c mind d hair e arm

20 The position of monarch is not something that is chosen by the people. It is ....

a inherit b generated c hereditary d descended e passed over

20 Missing words – "He said" etc

Put the following words into the correct sentences. Use each word once only.

boasted	pleaded	demanded
complained	snapped	shouted
suggested	stammered	inquired
whispered	insisted	explained

1 "What about going to the cinema tonight?" he ....

2 "Oh, but you can't go yet. You must stay for another drink at least," she
....

3 "Can you tell me where she lives?" .... the policeman.

4 "I want my money back!" .... the irate housewife.

5 "Oh, will you two shut up!" .... the mother to her two
children.

6 "I love you, Jane," he .... tenderly.

7 "I can play ten musical instruments," she ....

8 "Help! I can't swim! Help!" .... the girl as she went under
the water for the second time.

9 "You see, darling, it's like this," .... the girl's fiancé. "I just
can't afford to get married at the moment."

10 "Please don't kill me!" .... the girl as the hi-jacker pointed
his gun at her.

11 "It's not fair," .... the girl to her mother. "I never get
invited to parties."

12 "W...w...will you m...m...marry me?" he ....

21 Phrasal verbs 2

Replace the words in brackets in the following sentences with a suitable phrasal verb. (Make any other necessary changes.)

let off	go off	fall out
go through with	turn away	go with
do up	put up with	get out of
turn out	go over	put up
come round	get round to	put off
take for	come apart	get through to

1 Do you think you could .... this work with me some
                       (examine)

  time, Pete?

2 The teacher suspected that one of the class had stolen the money, so he made
  them all .... their pockets.
       (empty)

3 You look upset, Sven. Have you and Inger ....
                                   (quarrelled)

  again?

4 I tried to have lunch at the Savoy yesterday, but was ....
                                          (refused admittance)

  because I wasn't wearing a tie.

5 Guess what, Sue? I was .... John Travolta last
                 (mistaken for)

  week. It was a great feeling!

6 Paul, do you think you could .... me .... for the night? It's a
                    (give me a place to sleep)

  bit too late to go home now.

7 Many things are so badly made nowadays that they often ....
  .... after only a few weeks.
  (break into pieces)

8 He was caught shop-lifting but since this was his first offence he was
.... with a warning.
(allowed to go free)

9 I didn't really want to play football on Saturday, but since there was no one else
to take my place I couldn't really .... it.
(escape from doing)

10 Could you help me .... this parcel, please, Tom?
(wrap)

11 I don't know how she .... him. She must have the
(tolerates)
patience of a saint.

12 You never listen to me, Eva, do you? It's impossible to ....
.... you these days!
(reach)

13 I think David's .... me. He hasn't told me he loves
(stopped liking)
me for over a week.

14 The girl was relieved when her boyfriend .... after
(regained consciousness)
having fainted half-way through the Pop Concert.

15 I like your blouse, Sally. It .... your skirt.
(matches)

16 I know you find the course boring, Pauline, but since you've started it you might
as well .... it.
(complete)

17 The only thing that .... me .... getting married is the thought
(discourages me from)
of having to sleep in the same room as someone else.

18 I keep meaning to write to my parents but I'm so busy nowadays that I can't seem
to .... it.
(find the time to do)

22 What is it used for?

Read through the sentences and fill in the missing words.

1 A short nail or pin with a flat head that you press into a board or wall to hold a notice or picture in place. (2 words)
2 Very small metal or plastic cap put on the finger to protect it while sewing.
3 A covering put over a tea-pot to keep the contents warm. (2 words)
4 An instrument with a pendulum used by musicians to give them a steady beat.
5 Something used for looking at distant objects since they appear much closer through these.
6 A metal tool used to undo nuts.
7 An instrument you look into which is used to make very small things seem much larger so that they can be examined.
8 A small piece of plastic or tortoise-shell held in the fingers, used to play a guitar—especially electric guitars or guitars with steel strings.
9 A tool for making holes in paper, leather, metal, etc. The one for paper usually makes four holes at the same time.
10 A container with a lid used for holding rubbish until it can be taken away.
11 An instrument in the home used for blowing air into a fire to make it burn quickly.
12 A kitchen utensil shaped like a pan with lots of small holes. It is used for straining food.
13 A large vessel in a church, usually made of stone, that contains the water used for baptizing.
14 A horn-shaped instrument you speak into to make your voice carry out of doors. (It is not electric.)
15 You use this to help you draw straight lines.

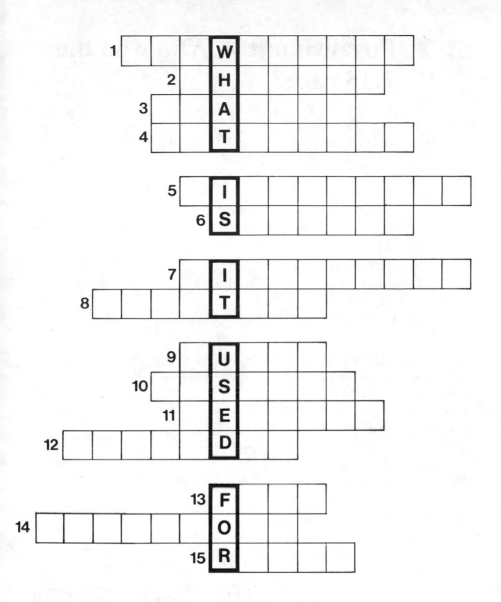

23 Puzzle it out – Who won the 2.15 race?

Here are the horses and betting odds for the 2.15 race at Kempton Park:

No.	Horse	Betting odds
1	ROYAL THRUST	25–1
2	DAVY LAD	2–1 (Fav.)
3	SPITTING IMAGE	10–1
4	RED RUM	5–1
5	WAR BONNET	10–1
6	FORT VULCAN	10–1
7	THE SONGWRITER	50–1
8	WILLY WHAT	50–1

Now read through the following sentences and see if you can work out who came 1st, 2nd and 3rd in the above race.

Fort Vulcan was in the lead with 2 furlongs to go.
There were only six finishers.
The horse that came second was an outsider (more than 20–1)
The Songwriter came last.
The favourite was in the lead with only 1 furlong to go.
The winning horse had odds of 10–1.
Royal Thrust fell at the third jump.
Red Rum passed the favourite half a furlong from the finish.
War Bonnet did not finish the race.
Horse number 6 came 5th.

3rd. .... 2nd. .... 1st. ....

(Note: 1 furlong = 1/8 English mile)

24 Add two letters

Add **two letters** to each of the following words (in any place) to form a new word. A clue is given to help you.

1	SIT	_SIXTH_	ordinal number
2	SEE		shop assistants do it
3	WAY		very tired
4	LAY		tall and very thin
5	CART		a vegetable
6	RAGE		a fruit
7	WAR		it's good for the garden
8	DAY		a short holdup
9	EAT		it comes to everyone
10	OR		part of an apple
11	RIPE		helps you cook
12	DEAR		dull or boring
13	COME		opposite of expenditure
14	HAY		most people would like to be this
15	ROW		a lot of people
16	TEN		frequently
17	SAW		you wear it
18	SAD		can be tiring to do this for a long time
19	BAND		it tastes nice, especially with coffee
20	RUG		popular game in Wales
21	SEEN		a country
22	CARE		you walk on it
23	SET		a piece of linen
24	STALE		used in an office
25	POLE		opposite of discourteous

33

25 Crime and punishment

Fill in the missing words in the sentences below. Choose from the following:

arrested	remanded in custody	defence
solicitor	evidence	barrister
verdict	proof	witness
fine	charged	testimony
juvenile delinquent	sentenced	arson
bail	Magistrate's Court	burglary
prosecution	probation	imprisonment
commit	embezzlement	
shoplifting	Crown Court	

1 The number of young people who .... crimes has risen sharply in recent years.
2 Another house was broken into last week. This is the third .... in the area in the past month.
3 The judge .... him to seven years' .... for armed robbery.
4 After twelve hours, the Jury finally reached its ....; the prisoner was guilty.
5 Although the police suspected that he had been involved in the robbery, since they had no definite .... there was nothing they could do about it.
6 He parked his car in the wrong place and had to pay a £20 parking ....
7 This is the fourth fire in the area recently. The police suspect ....
8 The shop decided to install closed-circuit television in an effort to combat the problem of ....
9 He was .... by the police outside a pub in Soho and .... with murder.
10 There are two criminal courts in Britain—the .... for minor offences and the .... for more serious ones.
11 A .... is a young person who breaks the law.

12 A .... is someone who sees a crime being committed.

13 The lawyer who prepares the case for his or her client prior to appearing in court is called a .... The lawyer who actually presents the case in court is called a ....

14 The sum of money left with a court of law so that a prisoner may be set free until his or her trial comes up is called ....

15 The bank manager admitted taking £250,000 of the bank's money during the previous five years. He was found guilty of ....

16 The witness held the Bible in her right hand and said: "I swear by Almighty God that the .... I shall give shall be the truth, the whole truth, and nothing but the truth."

17 The formal statement made by a witness in court is called a ....

18 If a person is ...., this means that he or she is put in prison before his or her trial comes up.

19 Since it was his first offence, he was not sent to prison but put on .... for 6 months.

20 At a trial, the barrister who speaks for the accused is called the Counsel for the ...., while the barrister who speaks against him is called the Counsel for the ....

26 Word building 2

Fill in the missing words in the following sentences by combining the verb in capital letters at the end of each sentence with a suitable adverb-particle (in, by, out, down, up, etc.)

Example: The Army tried unsuccessfully to <u>OVERTHROW</u>   THROW
         the Government.

1 There was a heavy .... yesterday   POUR
   afternoon which completely ruined the church Garden
   Party.

2 Although the splitting of the atom was one of the greatest   BREAK
   scientific .... of this century, there
   are many people who wish it had never happened.

3 The new .... has certainly made   PASS
   things a lot easier in the town centre since it has taken
   away all the through-traffic.

4 During a recent .... at a bank in   HOLD
   the West End of London, the raiders got away with
   £250,000

5 He was very .... when his cat was   SET
   run over.

6 There has been yet another .... of   BREAK
   cholera in Calcutta.

7 He completely went to pieces after the ....   BREAK
   of his marriage.

8 The firm's annual .... was in the   TURN
   region of £5,000,000.

9 The .... for tomorrow's weather is   LOOK
   very promising indeed, with temperatures well into the
   thirties forecast for most parts of the country.

10 The annual .... of students has de-   TAKE
   creased by 20 % in the last two years.

11 The factory's .... has increased   PUT
considerably in the past few years.

12 If you want to get involved with a married man, then it's   LOOK
your own .... But don't say I didn't
warn you!

13 The .... of the election is still not known.   COME

14 The .... of this disease is marked   SET
by a sudden loss of appetite coupled with a feeling of total
lethargy.

15. Wine, women and song were my brother's ....   FALL

16 I was late for work this morning because my car had a   BREAK
.... on the motorway.

17 There was a sudden .... of clapping   BURST
and cheering as he rose to receive the Nobel Peace Prize.

18 I hate being stuck behind lorries on country roads because   TAKE
they are so difficult to ....

19 My mother has just informed me that she will have to   GO
.... an operation next year, but she
won't tell me what for.

20 He felt very .... when she refused   CAST
to go out with him.

27 Crossword: things in the home

Look at the drawings and fill in the crossword below.

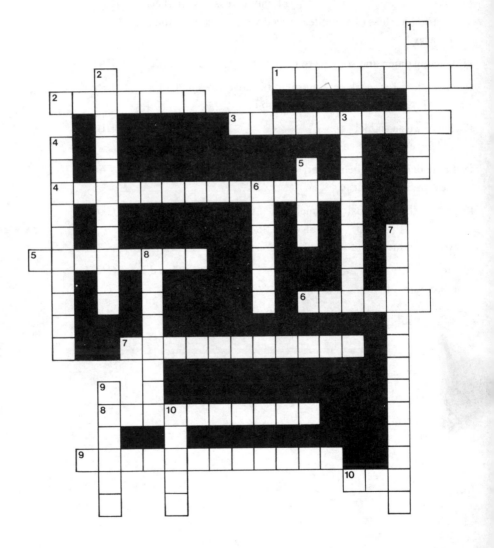

ACROSS

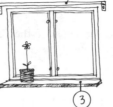

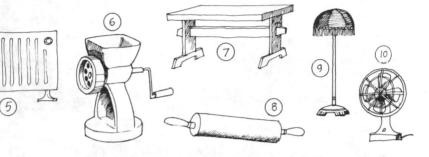

DOWN

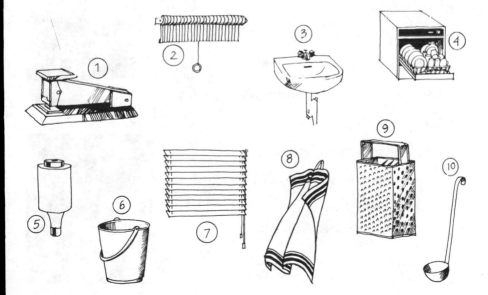

28 Classifications

Write one name for each of the following groups. Before starting, look at the example.

1 spring, summer, autumn, winter

2 carton, barrel, crate, bag

3 triangle, circle, square, rectangle

4 button, clasp, hook and eye, press studs

5 mahogany, pine, teak, birch

6 pheasant, partridge, grouse, rabbit

7 coffee, tea, chocolate, cocoa

8 sewing, knitting, crochet, embroidery

9 and, but, because, even though

10 bungalow, penthouse, hut, villa

11 1/2, 1/4, 3/4, 5/4

12 clubs, hearts, diamonds, spades

13 brass, bronze, pewter, chrome-nickel

14 astronomy, biology, botany, sociology

15 C.I.A., O.B.E., Ph. D., N.B.

16 amethyst, emerald, onyx, opal

17 ammonia, carbon dioxide, ether, methane

18 clay, salt, gypsum, lime

19 chronometer, grandfather clock, metronome, stopwatch

20 fish and chips, roast beef and Yorkshire pudding, bacon and eggs, shepherd's pie

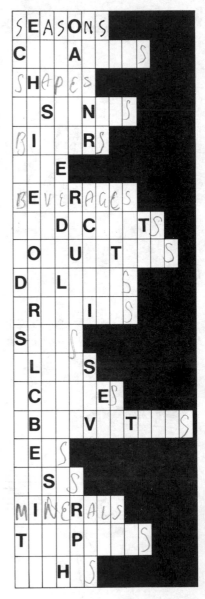

29 From Shore to Crash

Change the word SHORE into CRASH in sixteen stages, changing one or two letters at a time. (The number in brackets after each clue tells you how many letters of the preceding word need to be changed to form the new word.)

	S	H	O	R	E	
1						e.g. 2–0 (1)
2						to frighten (1)
3						to do with music (1)
4						a mammal (2)
5						a conjunction (1)
6						a sign of pleasure, happiness (2)
7						an odour (2)
8						foreigners often find it difficult to do this in English (1)
9						parents should try not to do this to their children (2)
10						a country (2)
11						a means of transport (2)
12						a .... of sand (1)
13						a fruit (2)
14						cows do this (1)
15						to rub out (2)
	C	R	A	S	H	

30 British and American English

Write down the missing British or American words.

AMERICAN ENGLISH	BRITISH ENGLISH
1 bill (money)	....
2	chimney
3 monkey wrench	....
4	handbag
5 flashlight	....
6	sellotape
7 yard	....
8	vest
9 tag	....
10	telegram
11 street musician	....
12	lamppost
13 blow-out	....
14	caravan
15 mortician	....
16	fire brigade
17 sideburns	....
18	pram
19 sucker	....
20	holiday

31 Missing words – "He walked" etc.

Put the following words into the correct sentences. Use each word once only.

stumbled	staggered	plodded
limped	strode	loitered
skipped	strolled	crept
marched	scampered	tramped

1 The angry man .... into the office and demanded to see the manager.

2 The soldiers proudly .... past the cheering crowds lining the streets.

3 The tired farmer .... home after a hard day's work in the fields.

4 The girl .... and fell as she was coming out of the office.

5 The mouse .... into its hole the moment it caught sight of the cat.

6 We'd have caught that train if you hadn't .... on the way!

7 The wounded man .... into the pub, crying, "Call an ambulance. I've been stabbed!"

8 The happy children .... along the road on their way to school.

9 We .... across the fields for miles and miles in search of mushrooms.

10 The lovers .... hand-in-hand through the park.

11 The lame man .... across the room.

12 The soldier .... silently towards the unsuspecting enemy guard.

32 Objects and things in the home 2

Write the number of each drawing next to the correct word.

duster   . . . . .
flex   . . . . .
toast rack   . . . . .
slide rule   . . . . .
headboard   . . . . .
pressure cooker . . . . .
continental quilt . . . . .
wrench   . . . . .
brace   . . . . .
bit   . . . . .
flannel   . . . . .
skirting board . . . . .

33 Prepositional phrases 2

Fill in the missing prepositions in the following sentences.

1 He went abroad .... *business*.
2 I was .... *a hurry*, so I chose a book .... *random*.
3 The tomb was discovered .... *accident*.
4 I can't get .... *touch* .... him. His telephone is ....
.... *order*.
5 Have you anyone .... *mind* .... the job?
6 He has collected over a thousand signatures .... *support* ....
his protest.
7 This is Mrs Brown. She's .... *charge* .... production.
8 Help! Help! My house is .... *fire*!
9 I'll have a beer. No, ... *second thoughts*, I'll have a whisky.
10 Hands up those .... *favour* .... going to Brighton.
11 Prepositions have to be learnt .... *heart*.
12 Mrs Brown has cleaned the house .... *top* .... *bottom*.
13 Thousands of people turned up for the concert .... *spite* ....
the bad weather.
14 Your work is quite good .... *the whole*.
15 He stepped on my toe .... *purpose*.
16 He is very extravagant and is always .... *debt*.
17 It is a good idea to *keep* .... *good terms* .... your teacher.
18 Although you have to give up a lot when you have children, it's probably worth
it .... *the long run*.
19 Let's go to the cinema this weekend .... *a change*.
20 I've just bought a new house .... *the outskirts* .... Brighton.

34 Colloquial expressions 2

Replace the words in brackets in the following sentences with a suitable colloquial expression from the list below.

on the house	like a bear with a sore	call it a day
given a good hiding	head	put your foot in it
I haven't a clue	given the sack	talking shop
for donkey's years	keep it quiet	out of the blue
pull your socks up	gets my goat	I can't make head or tail
	rings a bell	of it

1 I don't mind helping Charles with his English, but what ....
                                                               (annoys me)

.... is the way he seems to take my help for granted.

2 The news that the Prime Minister was going to resign came quite ....
                                                                (unexpectedly)

....

3 Well, I think we'd better .... now. We've done
                                (stop working)
as much as we can for one day.

4 What's wrong with Mr Barker this morning? He's ....
                                                (so irritable)

....

5 I don't think I've met her, but her name ....
                                              (sounds familiar)

6 Have you seen Mary? I've been looking for her all morning.

Sorry, John. ...., I'm afraid.
                        (I don't know)

7 Right everybody, place your orders. The drinks are ....
                                              (free)

8 I hate going to parties with groups of teachers. They seem to spend most of the

evening ....
                        (talking about their work)

9 By the way, you've heard about Tom, haven't you? He's been .... (dismissed

.... from his job)

10 I wonder what Julia's doing these days? I haven't seen her ....

.... (for a long time)

11 The child was .... by his father for telling lies. (beaten)

12 What's this supposed to mean? .... (I can't understand a word of it)

13 Incidentally, Rita and Jim have decided to get married. But .... (don't tell anyone)

.... — it's supposed to be a secret.

14 You really .... when you asked Pam how her cat was. Didn't you (blundered)

know it got run over last week?

15 You're going to have to .... if you want to pass (work much harder)

the exam.

35 Sounds

Fill in the correct words under each drawing.

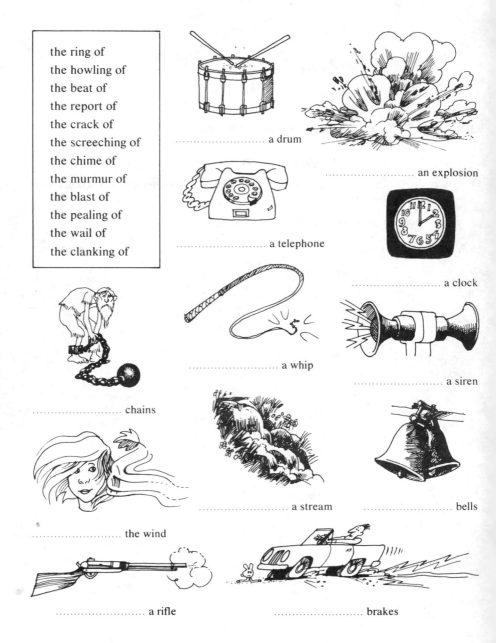

the ring of
the howling of
the beat of
the report of
the crack of
the screeching of
the chime of
the murmur of
the blast of
the pealing of
the wail of
the clanking of

.... a drum

.... an explosion

.... a telephone

.... a clock

.... a whip

.... a siren

.... chains

.... a stream   .... bells

.... the wind

.... a rifle   .... brakes

36 Which word is the same?

Underline the word which is closest in meaning to the first three words in each line. Number 1 has been done for you.

1 LOVE, LIKE, ENJOY — hope, hate, <u>adore,</u> raise
2 DECEIVE, FOOL, CHEAT — swindle, lose, lyre, drop
3 OBDURATE, STUBBORN, OBSTINATE — stable, adamant, envious, stale
4 EAGER, KEEN, ENTHUSIASTIC — careful, interesting, strong, zealous
5 TRY, ENDEAVOUR, ATTEMPT — undertake, make, construct, prove
6 CUNNING, CRAFTY, SLY — careful, artful, queer, inept
7 ORDER, COMMAND, DICTATE — claim, steer, decree, desire
8 REQUEST, BEG, ASK — assure, entreat, require, wish
9 WEALTHY, RICH, PROSPEROUS — affluent, noble, destitute, mean
10 DISLIKE, HATE, LOATHE — vomit, scour, abhor, stand
11 BRAVE, PLUCKY, BOLD — moody, feeble, strict, valiant
12 PROUD, VAIN, ARROGANT — conceited, stolen, heady, regal
13 ASTONISH, AMAZE, ASTOUND — favour, bewilder, increase, revise
14 WHOLE, TOTAL, SUM — amount, number, entirety, figure
15 EVENT, RESULT, CONSEQUENCE — reason, outcome, substitute, change
16 WEAK, FEEBLE, POWERLESS — stark, slow, impotent, able
17 REGION, AREA, ZONE — district, neighbour, suburb, border
18 STOUT, FAT, OBESE — shock, corpulent, stark, puny
19 DEPARTURE, WITHDRAWAL, RETREAT — arrival, entry, exodus, loss
20 KILL, SLAY, ASSASSINATE — load, slaughter, die, lead off

37 Fastenings/fasteners

Write the number of each drawing next to the correct word.

anchor	. . . . .
sling	. . . . .
clip	. . . . .
chain	. . . . .
stitch	. . . . .
joint	. . . . .
bolt	. . . . .
harness	. . . . .
handcuffs	. . . . .
cable	. . . . .
tacks	. . . . .
zip	. . . . .
rivet	. . . . .

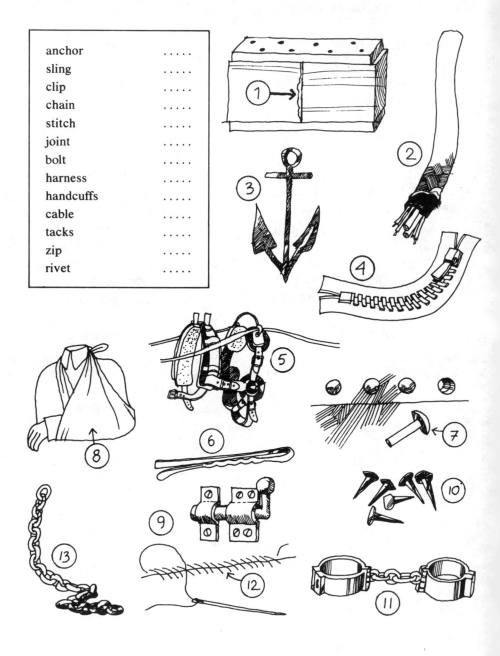

38 What is it part of?

Complete the following sentences by choosing an appropriate word from the ones on the right. Look at the example first.

1 A viewfinder is part of _A CAMERA_

2 A frame is part of ....

3 A rafter is part of ....

4 A pip is part of ....

5 A neck is part of ....

6 An eye is part of ....

7 A petal is part of ....

8 A prong is part of ....

9 A key is part of ....

10 A pawn is part of ....

11 A twig is part of ....

12 A beak is part of ....

13 A lapel is part of ....

14 An arm is part of ....

15 A blade is part of ....

16 A spine is part of ....

17 A flue is part of ....

18 A barrel is part of ....

19 A hem is part of ....

20 A sole is part of ....

a needle
a jacket
a book
a typewriter
a shoe
a chair
a window
a bottle
a knife
a roof
a camera
a dress
a fork
a chess set
a flower
a rifle
a bird
an orange
a branch
a chimney

39 Health words

Fill in the missing words in the sentences below. Choose from the following:

matron	antiseptic	Maternity Ward
surgeon	indigestion	general anaesthetic
family doctor	hay fever	measles
contagious	sedative	insomnia
midwife	x-ray	prescription
constipated	infectious	crutches
mumps	surgery	scald

1 In England, if you are ill you can either send for the .... or else go and visit him at his ....

2 The piece of paper you get from the doctor to take to the chemist's to obtain medicine, pills, etc. is called a ....

3 My wife is expecting a baby. She's in the .... of Buchanan Hospital at the moment.

4 Be careful with that boiling water; you might .... yourself!

5 If a disease is .... , it means it can be spread from person to person, especially in the air. On the other hand a .... disease is one which can only be spread from person to person by direct contact (or touch).

6 .... is an illness, something like a bad cold, which makes the person sneeze a lot. It is caused by breathing in pollen dust from plants.

7 A .... is a nurse who has received special training to help other women when they are giving birth to children.

8 His neck and mouth are swollen. I think he's got ....

9 Don't eat your food so quickly! You'll get ....

10 You'd better put some .... on that cut, just to be safe.

11 It must be .... She's got a fever, and look at all those small red spots on her face and body.

12 If you suffer from .... , your doctor may recommend taking sleeping tablets.

13 I think I'm .... I haven't been able to go to the toilet properly for days.

14 When she broke her leg, she had to go around on .... for several weeks afterwards.

15 You may have broken one of your ribs. I think we'd better take an .... , just to make sure.

16 A .... is a doctor whose job is to perform operations.

17 She was in such a state when her son died that the doctor gave her a .... to help calm her down.

18 Before you have an operation, you are usually given a .... to make you unconscious so that you will not feel any pain during it.

19 The woman in charge of a hospital is called the .... She has control over all the nurses. (But not the doctors!)

40 What are the questions?

Look at the following drawings then write down what the missing questions and answers are. The questions you will have to make up yourself but you can choose the answers from the ones below.

a No, I'd better not, thanks. I'm driving.

b No, of course not. I've only just arrived myself.

c I can't, I'm afraid. I'm already married.

d I'm sorry, but there's no one called John living here. You must have got the wrong number.

e No, it's all right, thank you. I can manage.

f Er . . . almost three.

g Not too bad, thanks. But I don't really like flying.

h I'm sorry, I'm a stranger here too.

i Yes, two lumps, please.

j Well, we were thinking of going to Poland for a change. It was so crowded last year in Spain.

k Er . . . it's the 5th I think.

l No, thanks. I've given it up.

41 Idioms of comparison

There are many short comparisons used in English to make the language more vivid and clear. Below are thirty of the most common ones. Complete each of them with a suitable word or words. Choose from the following:

a bat	chalk from cheese	mustard	the nose on your face
brass	a lord	life	the grave
a berry	a fiddle	a feather	a fox
a bee	a pancake	a hatter	a rock
a bell	a daisy	the hills	toast
a cucumber	gold	a church mouse	two peas in a pod
a doornail	nails	a picture	
a post	lead	clockwork	

1 As mad as ....
2 As flat as ....
3 As dead as ....
4 As heavy as ....
5 As light as ....
6 As regular as ....
7 As blind as ....
8 As different as ....
9 As clear as ....
10 As plain as ....
11 As like as ....
12 As cunning as ....
13 As hard as ....
14 As busy a ....
15 As keen as ....
16 As poor as ....
17 As steady as ....
18 As deaf as ....
19 As fit as ....

20 As pretty as ....
21 As bold as ....
22 As drunk as ....
23 As cool as ....
24 As warm as ....
25 As old as ....
26 As fresh as ....
27 As large as ....
28 As silent as ....
29 As good as ....
30 As brown as ....

42 Make or Do

Put the following words and phrases under the correct heading.
(There are fifteen under each).

a journey, progress, business, harm, a speech, one's best, a will, a mistake, fun of
someone, the garden, a good job, a complaint, the shopping, arrangements, a favour,
a bargain, the washing-up, repairs, the beds, a fuss, one's duty, someone a good
turn, an exercise, a nuisance of oneself, an effort, one's hair, an impression, homework, an examination, a profit.

MAKE	DO

43 Jobs

Fill in the missing jobs by looking at the list of words associated with each one.
Example: score, orchestra, baton, concert hall   CONDUCTOR

1 make-up, costume, script, props

2 typewriter, shorthand, telephone, filing cabinet

3 drill, denture, filling, mouth mirror

4 easel, canvas, palette, studio

5 stethoscope, scalpel, surgery, hypodermic

6 pipes, spanner, tap, blowlamp

7 bricks, trowel, hod, plumb-line

8 chalk, duster, homework, blackboard

9 barn, tractor, manure, plough

10 vestments, Host, crucifix, chalice

11 screwdriver, fuse, insulating tape, flex

12 saw, plane, chisel, try square

13 sewing-machine, pattern, pins, dummy

14 tripod, telephoto lens, darkroom, enlarger

15 typewriter, manuscript, proofs, best-seller

16 sack, uniform, pillar-box, letters

17 bench, beaker, test-tube, Bunsen burner

18 helmet, uniform, truncheon, handcuffs

19 hose, hydrant, ladder, extinguisher

20 hospital, thermometer, medicine, uniform

44 Cartoons

In the following cartoons, tha captions (i.e. the words that go with a cartoon) have got mixed up so that each cartoon has been printed with the wrong caption under it. Work out the correct caption for each cartoon.

Cartoon		Correct caption	Cartoon		Correct caption
1	–	....	6	–	....
2	–	....	7	–	....
3	–	....	8	–	....
4	–	....	9	–	....
5	–	....	10	–	....

5 LISTEN, THEY ARE PLAYING OUR TUNE.

6 CAN I RUN YOU HOME?

7 BUT WHAT MAKES YOU THINK THE BANANA DIET'S NOT WORKING, MRS BRIGHT?

8 HE'S ALWAYS BEEN A BIG FAN OF MICHELANGELO.

9 THERE MUST BE AN EASIER WAY TO KILL THEM, FRED!

10 IT'S THE COMMUTING THAT REALLY GETS ME DOWN.

45 Bits and pieces

Write the number of each drawing next to the correct word.

roundabout	.....
knitting needle	.....
nappy	.....
roof tiles	.....
scaffolding	.....
kerb	.....
firework	.....
music stand	.....
skipping rope	.....
telegraph pole	.....
parting	.....
drain	.....
pawn	.....
skylight	.....
udder	.....
gutter	.....
crutches	.....
cuff	.....
straw	.....
plimsoll	.....

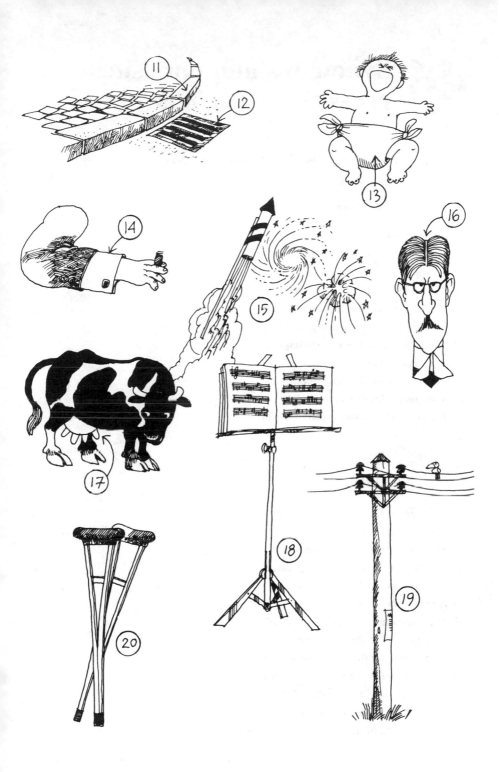

46 Synonyms and opposites crossword: various words

Read through the sentences below and fill in the crossword.

ACROSS

1 The opposite of the noun **profit**.
2 The opposite of the adjective **sweet**.
3 The opposite of the noun **exit**.
4 The opposite of the adjective **brave**.
5 A synonym for the verb **to boast**.
6 The opposite of the noun **punishment**.
7 The opposite of the verb **to improve**.
8 The opposite of the noun **landlord**.
9 A synonym for the adverb **especially**.
10 A synonym for the verb **to allow**.
11 The opposite of the adjective **useful**.

DOWN

1 A synonym for the verb **to receive**.
2 A synonym for the verb **to hide**.
3 The opposite of the verb **to admit**.
4 A synonym for the noun **argument**.
5 A synonym for the noun **mistake**.
6 A synonym for the verb **to hate**.
7 The opposite of the adjective **fertile**.
8 A synonym for the adjective **eager**.
9 A synonym for the adjective **naughty**.
10 A synonym for the verb **to disappear**.
11 The opposite of the verb **to praise**.
12 A synonym for the noun **cure**.
13 The opposite of the verb **to accept**.

47 Missing words – "A breath of", etc.

Put the following words into the correct sentences. Use each word once only.

stroke	breath	pinch
clap	attack	whiff
stretch	spell	plot
hint	shock	flash
wink	speck	gust

1 Just before the curtain went up, the actor suddenly developed a frightening .... of nerves.

2 I'm so tired. I didn't get a .... of sleep last night.

3 I know he sounds very convincing, but if I were you I'd take everything he says with a .... of salt.

4 I had a fantastic .... of luck last weekend. I picked up a genuine Stradivarius violin for only £25.

5 As he was walking past the building site he got a tiny .... of dust in his eye.

6 We've been having a marvellous .... of warm weather lately.

7 The neighbours must be eating garlic again. I just got a .... of it as I passed their door.

8 They have just opened a new .... of motorway between Brighton and London.

9 The sky was very black and a sudden .... of lightning made them all jump. They jumped even more when it was followed by a loud .... of thunder.

10 It's so stuffy in here. I really must go outside for a quick .... of fresh air.

11 There is a 3-acre .... of land for sale next to my house.

12 He was a tall, well-built man with a .... of red hair.

13 I was working at my desk when a sudden .... of wind blew all my papers onto the floor.

14 Now remember, Dave, send for the police at the slightest .... of trouble.

48 Newspaper misprints

In each of the following extracts from a newspaper there is a misprint. Underline the word which is wrong and also write down which word should have been used instead (see example).

1 Pamela Smith has been awarded the R.S.P.C.A. bronze medal for rescuing a <u>car</u> trapped up a tree. (.......*CAT*..................)

2 Some members of the Bulgarian secret police accepted brides in connection with the shipments. (.................................)

3 Part-time assistant required for sweat shop in Bexhill. (.................................)

4 Mature and considerable lady required to provide companionship to elderly lady. (.................................)

5 Mr Chris A. Gibson of New Zealand spoke next. His was also a humorous address, full of amusing antidotes. (.................................)

6 For Sale: Satan wedding dress, £30. (.................................)

7 He became champion by eating most of his main rivals. (.................................)

8 The Planning Board wants to make the village of Little Hampton a conversation area. (.................................)

9 This is a very serious offence which we shall have to deal with severely, as a detergent to anyone in the same mind. (.................................)

10 Window, mid-50s, youthful outlook, seeks company of tall, educated gentleman. (.................................)

11 With escalating fuel bills it is essential that your home is properly insulted. (.................................)

12 Father O'Connor, who is appearing in a show on behalf of the hospital, only sins for charity. (.................................)

13 She lectures on nutrition and health. But they say she is inconsistent and will eat five deserts in a sitting. (.................................)

14 Unlike most cats, Mrs P. explained, hers—owing to an eye injury—could hardly pee at all in the dark. (.................................)

15 Both were smartly dressed in three-piece suites. (.................................)

16 A bicycle worth £130 has been stolen from a mouse in Bolton. (.................................)

17 Fully killed mechanic required for busy garage. (.................................)

18 The problem of preventing violence in classrooms is a far wider one. Capital punishment is allowed in most schools but teachers are reluctant to use it. (.................................)

19 The farmer, who asked not to be named, said: "I was moving the lawn when I heard the plane go over." (..................................)

20 Jane met her husband while on holiday in Cyprus. "Chris was a member of the United Nations peach keeping force out there." (..................................)

21 Gale warnings have been issued for all land and sea areas, and guests of 78 m.p.h. were recorded off Dungeness. (..................................)

22 Cooked school meals are to be scraped next September by Bromley Council. (..................................)

23 Have your Christmas dinner with us in our intimate restaurant with log fires burning and good wood being served. (..................................)

24 A crucifix, given by Mr York to the church, was a welding present to his parents. (..................................)

25 TO LET: Furnished flat, £60 per month (rats inclusive). (..................................)

49 Colloquial expressions 3

Replace the words in brackets in the following sentences with a suitable colloquial expression from the list below.

get butterflies in my stomach	blowing his own trumpet	let the cat out of the bag
pulling my leg	hold my tongue	pig-headed
for a song	an out-and-out	he wouldn't say 'Boo' to a goose
smell a rat	as right as rain	cheesed off
to keep a straight face	down the drain	
	get on like a house on fire	

1 I see John's .... again. I've just
                         (boasting)

  heard him telling everyone he's the best tennis player in the County.

2 We were hoping to keep our engagement a secret, but my mother ....
                                            (told

  ....
  everyone about it)

3 I always .... before an interview.
                      (feel nervous)

4 We all found it difficult .... when
                         (not to laugh)

  we noticed that our teacher had forgotten to do up the zip on his trousers.

5 Well, that's £5 .... I told you that
                   (wasted)

  play wasn't worth seeing!

6 I must say that I found it hard to ....
                                (remain silent)

  when he started saying all those horrible things about foreigners.

7 You're not frightened of Mr Biggs, are you? ....
                                (He's very timid really)

  ....

8 I believed Ian when he told me he'd lost his job, but I later found out from Inger

that he was only ....
                          (joking)

9 You look a bit ...., John. What's
                          (fed up)

the matter?

10 The holiday was .... disaster. So
                          (a complete)

many things went wrong that it would take me all day to tell you about it.

11 I got a 1981 Jaguar the other day ....
                                        (very cheaply)

The owner was going abroad, so he just wanted to sell it quickly.

12 My wife will never admit that she's wrong, even when she knows she is. She's

so ....
                          (stubborn)

13 Just keep him at home today, Mrs Brown, and he'll be ....
                                                            (perfectly all right)

.... by tomorrow

14 I really like my mother-in-law. We, ...
                                        (have a really good relationship)

15 I though she was the new secretary, but I began to ....
                                                          (become suspicious)

.... when I found her going through coat pockets in the

cloakroom.

50 Words to describe (temporary) moods, states and feelings

Put the following words into the correct sentences. Use each word once only.

sympathetic	winded	terrified	embarrassed
depressed	peckish	pregnant	stiff
drowsy	offended	giddy	despondent
homesick	relieved	sober	preoccupied
tense	weary	nostalgic	disappointed
hoarse	faint	disgusted	dejected
furious	upset	thrilled	
amazed	listless	unconscious	

1 My father was .... when I told him that I had crashed his car. I don't think I have ever seen him so angry.

2 After walking for 6 hours, we were so .... that we couldn't go on.

3 I always feel .... when I look down from the top of a high building.

4 My legs are really .... after all that running we did yesterday.

5 The boxer hit his opponent so hard that he was knocked ....

6 I feel a bit .... Do you mind if I help myself to a sandwich?

7 Alison was very .... when she heard that her mother had been taken to hospital.

8 When I first moved to Sweden I felt very .... — I missed England so much.

9 She was really .... when she heard that she had got the job.

10 I spoke to her, but she was too .... to notice me.

11 After singing all evening I found that I could scarcely talk afterwards—my voice was really ....

12 My sister was .... when her friend's Alsatian started
   barking at her.
13 She was very .... when I told her that I had lost my
   job.
14 I felt really .... when my mother started telling my
   girlfriend about the strange habits I used to have when I was a child.
15 The centre-forward was temporarily .... when he
   was kicked in the stomach going for the ball.
16 My husband was really thrilled when I told him that I was.........................
17 When Mary refused to go out with him, John felt really ....
18 You look ...., Alan. Cheer up! Things can't be that
   bad.
19 The sight of blood always makes me feel ....
20 Listening to 'She Loves You' by the Beatles made me feel very
   ....
21 She felt very .... when the doctor told her that it
   wasn't cancer.
22 Lying in the sun made me feel very ....
23 Amanda was so .... when she failed her driving-test.
   She had really set her heart on passing it first time.
24 The hotel room was so dirty that I felt thoroughly ....
   and complained to the manager.
25 My cousin was deeply .... when I didn't invite him to my wedding.
26 When we heard that he had passed the exam we were all ....
   No one had thought he would do it.
27 I hate the heat—it makes me feel so .... I just don't
   want to move or do anything.
28 He told me that when his wife left him he felt really ....
   Life didn't seem worth living, and he even contemplated committing suicide.
29 I felt very .... before the interview. But once I actually started talking I began to relax.
30 Although he was perfectly .... when he arrived at the
   party, by 11.30 he was as drunk as everyone else.

Answers

TEST 1

bat	5
donkey	8
octopus	11
wolf	6
elk	7
fox	9
rhinoceros	12
hedgehog	2
reindeer	3
hippopotamus	1
squirrel	10
tortoise	4

TEST 2

1 trip
2 voyage
3 run
4 flight
5 tour
6 travel
7 excursion
8 expedition
9 journey
10 cruise
11 package tour
12 outing

TEST 3

1(c) skylight
2(a) use
3(c) intention
4(d) denied
5(b) core
6(d) spinster
7(a) cat's eyes
8(b) gap
9(d) minutes
10(e) head over heels
11(a) paw

12(b) faintest
13(b) sprained
14(c) advised
15(c) vivid
16(a) resumed
17(c) peeling
18(a) critically
19(e) needles
20(b) upset

TEST 4

1 do him in
2 gone off
3 gave him away
4 goes back to
5 call on
6 cut up
7 getting me down
8/ gone down with
9 look it up
10 get at
11 went out
12 getting on for
13 take away
14 gone down
15 took to
16 turned it down
17 look in
18 take off

TEST 5

1 a versatile
2 a convivial
3 a magnanimous
4 a greedy
5 a gullible
6 a chauvinistic
7 an illiterate
8 a bilingual
9 an indefatigable

10 an erudite
11 a scintillating
12 a vivacious

TEST 6

thigh bone	9
collarbone	3
kneecap	10
skull	1
shin bone (tibia)	12
wrist bones	8
breastbone	5
spine/backbone	2
shoulder blade	4
hipbone	7
fibula	11
rib	6

TEST 7

1 prison
2 piano
3 newspaper
4 bed
5 golf
6 car
7 astrology
8 boxing
9 watch
10 roof
11 cat
12 camera
13 theatre
14 aeroplane
15 window
16 funeral
17 chess
18 castle
19 rugby
20 farm

TEST 8

1 scenery
2 landscape
3 scene
4 country
5 highlands
6 countryside
7 rural
8 nature
9 bush
10 setting
11 environment
12 view

TEST 9

1 disability
2 basically
3 artistic
4 unreasonable
5 actions
6 applicable
7 bloodshot
8 comparatively
9 confidential
10 continually
11 disobedience
12 classifying
13 indefensible
14 mistaken
15 imprisonment
16 partially
17 disqualified
18 widespread
19 precision
20 headstrong

TEST 10

Across
1 incredible
2 industrious
3 mean
4 considerate
5 rude
6 temporary

7 blunt
8 conceited
9 accidental
10 huge

Down
1 irritated
2 transparent
3 obstinate
4 odd
5 scarce
6 compulsory
7 tiny
8 affluent
9 dependable
10 exciting

TEST 11

1 recognised
2 gazed
3 caught a glimpse of
4 distinguish
5 Look at
6 glanced
7 peeped
8 glared
9 scrutinised
10 staring
11 eyed
12 peered
13 noticing
14 watch
15 catch his eye
16 observing

TEST 12

1 company
2 tribe
3 board
4 suite
5 flock
6 bunch
7 litter
8 team
9 staff

10 crowd
11 herd
12 swarm
13 set
14 crew
15 pack
16 shoal
17 fleet
18 suit
19 bundle
20 flight

TEST 13

nut	2
butter-dish	3
coal scuttle	12
sieve	5
box of tissues	10
bolt	1
rubbish-bin	9
washer	4
table-mat	6
chopper	11
draining-board	8
mantlepiece	7

TEST 14

1 black and blue all over
2 got into hot water
3 hard up
4 at loggerheads
5 stuck up
6 dead beat
7 gave me the cold shoulder
8 make ends meet
9 was a bit out of sorts
10 flogging a dead horse
11 hit the roof
12 few and far between
13 get a move on
14 cats and dogs
15 It sticks out a mile

TEST 15

1 in
2 at
3 in ... At
4 out of
5 in
6 on
7 on ... of
8 in
9 at ... of
10 in
11 at
12 in
13 in
14 by
15 by
16 in
17 for
18 for
19 by
20 in

TEST 16

1 Field Marshal
2 Secretary-General
3 producer
4 foreman
5 manager
6 headmaster/head-
   mistress
7 abbot
8 captain
9 curator
10 governor
11 butler
12 Principal
13 chairman
14 Vice-Chancellor
15 umpire
16 Prime Minister
17 chief/chieftain
18 Managing Director
19 Mother Superior
20 leader
21 warden
22 choirmaster

23 President
24 editor
25 matron

TEST 17

1 binary
2 tricycle
3 century
4 soloist
5 bigamist
6 duet
7 pentagon
8 decade
9 biplane
10 fortnight
11 duel
12 monologue
13 ambidextrous
14 twins
15 centipede
16 binoculars
17 unicorn
18 quartet
19 coalition
20 triplets

TEST 18

1 crippled
2 altered
3 non-flammable
4 defective
5 blinked
6 comic
7 trained
8 electrical
9 childish
10 rumour
11 collaborate
12 Technical
13 specially
14 disinterested
15 nil
16 possibility

17 disused
18 counsellor
19 room
20 shade
21 possibly
22 umpire
23 policy
24 steps
25 barrister
26 write-up
27 financial
28 morale
29 convenient
30 amenities

TEST 19

1(a) full up
2(d) waste
3(d) brand
4(c) perjury
5(b) keep
6(a) left
7(c) profit
8(b) prevent
9(d) estimated
10(c) order
11(e) short
12(d) write-up
13(b) clap
14(c) tough
15(a) else
16(c) gossip
17(b) plot
18(a) fine
19(b) leg
20(c) hereditary

TEST 20

1 suggested
2 insisted
3 inquired
4 demanded
5 snapped
6 whispered

7 boasted
8 shouted
9 explained
10 pleaded
11 complained
12 stammered

TEST 21

1 go over
2 turn out
3 fallen out
4 turned away
5 taken for
6 put me up
7 come apart
8 let off
9 get out of
10 do up
11 puts up with
12 get through to
13 gone off
14 came round
15 goes with
16 go through with
17 puts me off
18 get round to

TEST 22

1 drawing pin
2 thimble
3 tea cosy
4 metronome
5 binoculars
6 spanner
7 microscope
8 plectrum
9 punch
10 dustbin
11 bellows
12 colander
13 font
14 megaphone
15 ruler

TEST 23

1st   Spitting Image
2nd   Willy What
3rd   Red Rum

TEST 24

1 sixth
2 serve
3 weary
4 lanky
5 carrot
6 orange
7 water
8 delay
9 death
10 core
11 recipe
12 dreary
13 income
14 happy
15 crowd
16 often
17 shawl
18 stand
19 brandy
20 rugby
21 Sweden
22 carpet
23 sheet
24 stapler
25 polite

TEST 25

1 commit
2 burglary
3 sentenced ... impris-
  onment
4 verdict
5 proof
6 fine
7 arson
8 shoplifting
9 arrested ... charged

10 Magistrate's Court ...
   Crown Court
11 juvenile delinquent
12 witness
13 solicitor ... barrister
14 bail
15 embezzlement
16 evidence
17 testimony
18 remanded in custody
19 probation
20 defence ... prosecution

TEST 26

1 downpour
2 breakthroughs
3 by-pass
4 holdup
5 upset
6 outbreak
7 breakup
8 turnover
9 outlook
10 intake
11 output
12 lookout
13 outcome
14 onset
15 downfall
16 breakdown
17 outburst
18 overtake
19 undergo
20 downcast

TEST 27

Across
1 plate rack
2 trolley
3 window sill
4 scrubbing brush
5 radiator
6 mincer
7 coffee table

8   rolling pin
9   standard lamp
10 fan

Down
1   stapler
2   roller blind
3   washbasin
4   dishwasher
5   fuse
6   bucket
7   venetian blind
8   tea towel
9   grater
10 ladle

TEST 28

1   seasons
2   containers
3   shapes
4   fasteners
5   timbers
6   game
7   beverages
8   handicrafts
9   conjunctions
10 dwellings
11 fractions
12 suits
13 alloys
14 sciences
15 abbreviations
16 gems
17 gases
18 minerals
19 timepieces
20 dishes

TEST 29

1   score
2   scare
3   scale
4   whale
5   while

6   smile
7   smell
8   spell
9   spoil
10 Spain
11 train
12 grain
13 grape
14 graze
15 erase

TEST 30

American English
1   bill
2   smokestack
3   monkey wrench
4   purse
5   flashlight
6   Scotch tape
7   yard
8   undershirt
9   tag
10 wire
11 street musician
12 streetlight
13 blow-out
14 trailer
15 mortician
16 fire department
17 sideburns
18 baby carriage
19 sucker
20 vacation

British English
1   bank note
2   chimney
3   spanner
4   handbag
5   torch
6   sellotape
7   garden
8   vest
9   label
10 telegram
11 busker

12 lamppost
13 puncture
14 caravan
15 undertaker
16 fire brigade
17 sideboards
18 pram
19 lollipop
20 holiday

TEST 31

1   strode
2   marched
3   plodded
4   stumbled
5   scampered
6   loitered
7   staggered
8   skipped
9   tramped
10 strolled
11 limped
12 crept

TEST 32

duster	3
flex	11
toast rack	5
slide rule	6
headboard	1
pressure cooker	12
continental quilt	7
wrench	2
brace	9
bit	10
flannel	4
skirting board	8

TEST 33

1   on
2   in ... at
3   by

4   in ... with/out of
5   in ... for
6   in ... of
7   in ... of
8   on
9   on
10 in ... of
11 by
12 from ... to
13 in ... of
14 on
15 on
16 in
17 on ... with
18 in
19 for
20 on ... of

TEST 34

1   gets my goat
2   out of the blue
3   call it a day
4   like a bear with a sore head
5   rings a bell
6   I haven't a clue
7   on the house
8   talking shop
9   given the sack
10 for donkey's years
11 given a good hiding
12 I can't make head or tail of it
13 keep it quiet
14 put your foot in it
15 pull your socks up

TEST 35

the beat of a drum
the blast of an explosion
the ring of a telephone
the chime of a clock
the clanking of chains
the crack of a whip
the wail of a siren
the howling of the wind
the murmur of a stream
the pealing of bells
the report of a rifle
the screeching of brakes

TEST 36

1   adore
2   swindle
3   adamant
4   zealous
5   undertake
6   artful
7   decree
8   entreat
9   affluent
10 abhor
11 valiant
12 conceited
13 bewilder
14 entirety
15 outcome
16 impotent
17 district
18 corpulent
19 exodus
20 slaughter

TEST 37

anchor	3
sling	8
clip	6
chain	13
stitch	12
joint	1
bolt	9
harness	5
handcuffs	11
cable	2
tacks	10
zip	4
rivet	7

TEST 38

1   a camera
2   a window
3   a roof
4   an orange
5   a bottle
6   a needle
7   a flower
8   a fork
9   a typewriter
10 a chess set
11 a branch
12 a bird
13 a jacket
14 a chair
15 a knife
16 a book
17 a chimney
18 u rifle
19 a dress
20 a shoe

TEST 39

1   family doctor ... surgery
2   prescription
3   Maternity Ward
4   scald
5   infectious ...contagious
6   Hay fever
7   midwife
8   mumps
9   indigestion
10 antiseptic
11 measles
12 insomnia
13 constipated
14 crutches
15 x-ray
16 surgeon
17 sedative
18 general anaesthetic
19 matron

TEST 40

Suggested answers (others may be possible):

1   Could (can) I speak to John, please?
d   I'm sorry, but there's no one called John living here. You must have got the wrong number.
2   Would you like a cigarette? (Do you smoke?)
l   No, thanks. I've given it up.
3   What's the time, please?
f   Er...almost three.
4   Excuse me, can you tell me the way to (how to get to) Station Road, please?
h   I'm sorry, I'm a stranger here, too.
5   Would you like me to carry your suitcase? (Shall I carry your suitcase?)
e   No, it's all right, thank you. I can manage.
6   Where are you going for your holidays (this year/summer)?
j   Well, we were thinking of going to Poland for a change. It was so crowded last year in Spain.
7   I'm not late am I? (I do hope I'm not late.)
b   No, of course not. I've only just arrived myself.
8   Would you like a (another) drink?
a   No, I'd better not, thanks. I'm driving.
9   Did you have a good flight/journey?
g   Not too bad, thanks. But I don't really like flying.
10 What's the date?/Do you know what the date is?/What's today's date? /What's the date today?
k   Er...it's the 5th I think.
11 Do you take sugar?
i   Yes, two lumps, please.
12 Will you marry me?
c   I can't I'm afraid. I'm already married.

TEST 41

1   a hatter
2   a pancake
3   a doornail
4   lead
5   a feather
6   clockwork
7   a bat
8   chalk from cheese
9   a bell
10 the nose on your face
11 two peas in a pod
12 a fox
13 nails
14 a bee
15 mustard
16 a church mouse
17 a rock
18 a post
19 a fiddle
20 a picture
21 brass
22 a lord
23 a cucumber
24 toast
25 the hills
26 a daisy
27 life
28 the grave
29 gold
30 a berry

TEST 42

Make
a journey
progress
a speech
a will
a mistake
fun of someone
a complaint
arrangements
a bargain
the beds
a fuss
a nuisance of oneself
an effort
an impression
a profit

Do
business
harm
one's best
the garden
a good job
the shopping
a favour
the washing-up
repairs
one's duty
someone a good turn
an exercise
one's hair
homework
an examination

TEST 43

1   actor
2   secretary
3   dentist
4   artist
5   doctor
6   plumber
7   bricklayer
8   teacher
9   farmer

10 priest
11 electrician
12 carpenter
13 dressmaker
14 photographer
15 writer
16 postman
17 chemist
18 policeman
19 fireman
20 nurse

TEST 44

Cartoon	Correct caption
1	8
2	7
3	6
4	5
5	10
6	4
7	9
8	3
9	1
10	2

TEST 45

roundabout	7
knitting needle	10
nappy	13
roof tiles	4
scaffolding	9
kerb	11
firework	15
music stand	18
skipping rope	1
telegraph pole	19
parting	16
drain	12
pawn	6
skylight	5
udder	17
gutter	3
crutches	20

cuff	14
straw	8
plimsoll	2

TEST 46

Across
1 loss
2 sour
3 entrance
4 cowardly
5 brag
6 reward
7 deteriorate
8 tenant
9 particularly
10 permit
11 useless

Down
1 obtain
2 conceal
3 deny
4 row
5 error

TEST 48

Misprint	Correct word
1 car	cat
2 brides	bribes
3 sweat	sweet
4 considerable	considerate
5 antidotes	anecdotes
6 Satan	Satin
7 eating	beating
8 conversation	conservation
9 detergent	deterrent
10 Window	Widow
11 insulted	insulated
12 sins	sings
13 deserts	desserts
14 pee	see
15 suites	suits
16 mouse	house

6 detest
7 barren
8 keen
9 mischievous
10 vanish
11 criticise
12 remedy
13 reject

TEST 47

1 attack
2 wink
2 pinch
4 stroke
5 speck
6 spell
7 whiff
8 stretch
9 flash ... clap
10 breath
11 plot
12 shock
13 gust
14 hint

17	killed		skilled	
18	Capital		Corporal	
19	moving		mowing	
20	peach		peace	
21	guests		gusts	
22	scraped		scrapped	
23	wood		food	
24	welding		wedding	
25	rats		rates	

TEST 49

1	blowing his own trumpet	5	unconscious
2	let the cat out of the bag	6	peckish
3	get butterflies in my stomach	7	upset
4	to keep a straight face	8	homesick
5	down the drain	9	thrilled
6	hold my tongue	10	preoccupied
7	He wouldn't say 'Boo' to a goose	11	hoarse
8	pulling my leg	12	terrified
9	cheesed off	13	sympathetic
10	an out-and-out	14	embarrassed
11	for a song	15	winded
12	pig-headed	16	pregnant
13	as right as rain	17	dejected
14	get on like a house on fire	18	depressed
15	smell a rat	19	faint
		20	nostalgic
		21	relieved
		22	drowsy
		23	disappointed
		24	disgusted

TEST 50

		25	offended
		26	amazed
1	furious	27	listless
2	weary	28	despondent
2	giddy	29	tense
4	stiff	30	sober